THE MONEY FREE SOCIETY

A NEW SYSTEM

Bibliographische Information der Deutschen Nationalbibliothek verzeichnet diese Publikation in der Deutschen Nationalbibliographie; detaillierte bibliographische Daten sind im Internet über dnb.dnb.de abrufbar.

© 2016 Michael Kruse

Herstellung und Verlag: BoD-Books on Demand,Norderstedt

ISBN: 9783741238093

INDEX

1. CAPITALISM…………………………………………………………………page 4

2. FAILURES IN THE SYSTEM………………………………………….page 7

3. PATHWAY TO CHANGE……………………………………………….page 12

4. NEW VALUES………………………………………………………………page 14

5. RIGHTS AND DUTIES………………………………………………….page 15

6. POINT SYSTEM……………………………………………………………page 16

7. FAMILY………………………………………………………………………page 17

8. WORK…………………………………………………………………………page 18

9. HOUSING……………………………………………………………………page 20

10. FREE TIME…………………………………………………………………page 21

11. CLOSING REMARKS………………………………………………….page 22

1. CAPITALISM

Our capitalistic money system was I repeat was, the best economic system that was ever invented. Somebody had the idea that we could trade goods for cash money which was much more practical then trade business, where one could only trade goods for goods. The capitalistic system really got started in the first industrial revolution in the 1800s in Great Britain. The steam engine and the mechanical loom were invented and because of these inventions it was possible to shift from a mere crops economy to mass production in factories. The textile industry grew bigger and with George Stevensons invention of the steam locomotive in 1814, it was possible to travel to another place at a constant speed. The second industrial revolution started in the 1870s with the invention of many electrical devices. Industrial revolution number 3 is also known as the digital revolution it started at the end of the 20 century and accelerated our everyday lives with computers. All of these inventions and achievements were necessary to enable us to live in a modern society as we know today. To get back to the different system types: In the 1920s, fascism became popular in many European countries. Fascism is a right- wing, political system were the race doctrine plays an important role. The individual is not very important he places his demands behind those of the people. In fascism a totalitarian party rules, that steers the nation into being a united society that is indoctrinated to expand itself. The people are forced to annect other countries and enslave and destroy the inhabitants and in doing that, they enjoy more prosperity. At about the same time in Russia, which was later known as the main part of the Soviet Union, communism came into power. Communism says that the wealth belongs to the community. Everybody should work together to achieve prosperity, which sounds like a good idea. The problem in all communist countries is that they choose a centrally planned economy. The communist party manages the production of goods and controls the service economy. It turned out to be a very inefficient economic structure because first; the government decides when and what is to be produced and it leads to wrong decisions because the state workers either don't know very much about the topic, or they are too slow to react to necessary adjustments. Secondly because the individual feels he is not allowed to make his own decisions. He doesn't have a motive to go to work, because it's either meaningless or he doesn't see any self-interest in it. At the same time in the rest of the "free world", everybody was living in capitalism. It started to dawn on everyone that you could live much better in capitalism; there was prosperity, freedom, democracy and independence. The people in Europe gave up the communist system and it's only found nowadays in Cuba and North Korea where the populations are desperately poor and locked in. After the two World Wars capitalism was flourishing. Mostly in Europe and Asia everything had to be built up again. America had an economic boom after the Great Depression and became the biggest capitalistic superpower. Capitalism is an economic system where the most important goals are to achieve private property and higher capital resources. In Germany and other European countries we have social market economies. That is capitalism with social compensation. That means the social-weak and citizens in need are to be supported. They will be helped by means of money subsidies, primary care or social facilities. The idea is that work is to be taxed with a social insurance contribution and that everybody becomes the necessary social payments when he or she is in need.

2. FAILURES IN THE SYSTEM

The life we live could just go on the same way forever. The world would produce more wealth until nobody is sick, workless or starving. Since everybody has enough, nobody has to steal, rob or fight each other and the world would be a peaceful planet. We notice it is not like that but why?

a.) TECHNOLOGY

Because of the industrial revolutions we can make machines, cars and appliances much more efficiently. The crops industry was never capable to harvest so much like it does now, thanks to chemical fertilizers, hugh harvesters and packaging production line work. But what is good on the one side is bad on the other. To do the job, we need less workers, that is why we have more half-time jobs, limited work contracts and temporary employment. Employees have to be flexible and accept long ways to work. We are working in the long run against our own technological achievements and when everything gets digitalized and there are more working robots, than a lot us are going to be unemployed.

b.) SOCIAL ASPECTS

During the Cold War there were two different systems (capitalism and communism) and they were not only in military but also in social support issues competitors. Especially in East and West Germany both sides tried to look more attractive to the people. But it became clear that the Eastblock and USSR with their centrally planned economies were not able to satisfy their societies needs for consuming and independence. After the fall of communism, most countries started slowly reducing their social standards to stay competitive in the world markets. Thanks to globalization, companies can pick in which country they want to produce in. It is possible to make profits where there are low salaries, poor work standards and a lack of environment protection laws. If it´s about hourly wage rate, working hours, unemployment benefits, or property taxes, the communities and countries have to make it worse for the population. The same thing is when the conglomerates have to pay tax on profit because they are global players they shift their losses and profits from one branch to another until they barely have to pay anything. Most of the money made is not through "hard" work like when something is produce but from interest and inheritance. This is a burden to a countries treasury, because it can't give enough social benefits to the general public. A couple of days ago I heard in the radio that half of the population are only going to get a security pension as high as the social welfare-standard and that there is a discussion about a raise of the pension age to 70 years. That is definitely not the end of the road, like a politician said "If something is for sure, it's the pensions" he didn't say though at what age and how much. In Germany we have a specific problem with demographic change, the population lives longer because of high life standards (nutrition, healthcare) and at the same time, less children are being born. This has a big impact on the pension system and is becoming way too expensive. For the arms-producing countries, war is very profitable, the war economy gets generated and when it's over the winners get more influence and power as they build up the country again. Every citizen needs access to medical care, a new home, food, infrastructure etc. That is the paradoxical thing, that a peaceful world is actually bad for capitalism. Because of globalization the BRIC and Third-World countries are catching up faster to America and Europe and that's why we are reaching over capacities in a lot of things. When various countries try to standardize the markets with trade agreements like TTIP, then the decimation of social benefits will accelerate. Another aspect in the globalized economy is that money, goods and raw materials can be shipped all around the world to make higher returns. What isn't allowed to move everywhere, are the people, they try to follow the money and want to live somewhere where they can have a good life. Because this disadvantage most of the people are the losers in globalization, they become so-called economic refugees who try to immigrate from Third-World countries to America and Europe. They want the same high life standards that we have in the western world. We have a growing demand for raw materials and market claims and that is why we have armed conflicts and wars that make more people homeless and force them to look for a new place to live.

c.) ENVIRONMENT

If it was possible that we could settle on other planets like portrayed in a lot of science-fiction movies, than our damage to the environment wouldn't be a big issue. The problem is, we only have this one planet earth. Because of our expansionist politics and capitalistic system we are harming our environment more and more. We have already reached some peaks (oilpeak, soilpeak) that means, our resources are diminishing. At the same time we are polluting our globe, which leads to higher earth temperatures, climate catastrophes, less clean water and the extinction of animals and plants. The problem is climate change cannot be determined by a single event, it's a slow process: The Australian Great Barrier Reef is bleaching out, a rhino species goes extinct, longer droughts in Spain etc. Like the story about the frog in the pot: A frog jumped into a pot of water, noticed it was hot and jumped out right away, the next day he jumped into the pot and it was cold so he stayed inside. What he didn't notice was that the pot was on the stove and it was turned on. Because the water only got warm slowly, he stayed inside until he got cooked. Most people are noticing that our living space is doing worse and that's why the economy and government are always trying to do some touching-up on, like more "green" products, higher environment standards or the withdrawl from the nuclear energy program in Germany. But it won't be enough to save our planet because our capitalistic system is going in the wrong direction, through improvements we're going slower but we're still going down.

Do we want to always have to live faster and our problems to get bigger? I always campare capitalism to the board game Monopoly: At the beginning everyone gets the same amount of money and it's fun to buy streets and build houses and hotels, but as the game goes on there are 1 or 2 players that keep getting more and if you're one of them than the game just gets better, you can't collect cash and build hotels fast enough. If you belong to the majority of the players though, than the game gets more expensive and you have to pay mortgages and try to survive. At the end of the game one player has all the streets, the others can't pay their debts and it is game over. We can see that a lot of people don't want to play the capitalistic game anymore they come logically from the lower or middle class. Nowadays you can join a counter movement anywhere it could be called

Occupy, Greenpeace, Pegida, ATTAC or rally for peace. Some turn radical right –or left wing (Antifa), others even search for a meaning in life in a terroristic organization or state like ISIS, where they are manipulated for someones claims of power. It doesn't matter if it's a right-wing, left-wing, conservative, liberal, populist or an ecological political party, when they come to power they have to give the markets more freedom and cut social benefits to keep the country competitively viable. Everybody is in a competition against each other: Young against old, rich against poor, man against woman, humans versus nature and the fight is getting tougher. Is there a solution to all these problems?

3. PATHWAY TO CHANGE

To get in the right direction we need some course corrections. The government should act and not just react to situations. The good thing in Germany and other European countries is that we still have a pretty good social infrastructure, which should be expanded and not eliminated: Free access to health-and foster care, free education and that everyone has a right to social housing with a certain size. Public transportation systems should be extended and made more affordable. You probably say "Sounds like a good idea but how do we pay for all that?" All products should be highly taxed with an environment tax for example. In exchange the products should be more sturdy and robust, they should function as long as possible. When something does get broken, than it should be cheaper to repair it and not like nowadays that things are just thrown away and a new one is bought. The way products with a Made in Germany or Made in U.S.A. seal are known for good quality, it should be that the products are known to be the most environmental friendly, most long-lasting on the market. It is also important that the goods and packaging are returnable or biodegradable and if it's possible from the area (short transport routes). Organic food should be subsidized and meat should be more expensive because of its hugh need of water and animal feed. This isn't going to be cheap of course but the products could be paid by a monthly installment with lifetime guarantee, you wouldn't just buy a brand it's a whole new lifestyle. To be able to fill the state treasuries the rich have to contribute more through higher wealth-, financial transaction-and inheritance taxes. At the same time tax evasion in tax havens and offshore companies should be liable to result in criminal proceedings.

4. NEW VALUES

We all know that we have to stop our capitalistic money system that depends on a consume -and throw away mentality but how? We need a new system where technology and automation are a needful help at work and in our everyday lives. Not like it is today where our technological achievements force us to work more and faster to make ends meet and pushes us into precarious work contracts. We need something that benefits our social life and gives us more time for friendships, clubs and raising a family. Social help needs to be secured by the state so that we don't have to worry if we have enough money to pay for health – and nursing care, mobility and rent. And last but not least we need something that relieves our environment and nature and not a system that harms and destroys it. It should make our lives easier but at the same time push us to develop ourselves further. Just leaving our modern world and going back to Stone Age, isn't an option of course. We humans always need to have a goal to strive for, what is now money and consumption. I was thinking what is getting more and more precious nowadays and the answer is: Spare time. We are getting speeded up from work, everyday life, traffic and life planning, everything has to be faster and more efficient, which results in us not being able to really enjoy anything anymore because we're always stressed out and that makes us unhappy and sick. A society where spare time and not money and consumption the most important thing is, is much more logical. Goods should not be made to make maximum profit, but to make our lives easier, considering that they are high quality, long-living, ecological and regional. How could a system like this work?

5. RIGHTS AND DUTIES

RIGHTS: Every citizen becomes a card with their data (name, address, birthday and credit). With the card one has access to free education, health –and nursery care. Public transportation and telecommunications are free of charge. Everyone is also entitled to have a certain amount of square meter living space. Everybody has the right to have work.

DUTIES: Everyone has to either work, go to school or do further education. If this is not possible than you have to do a therapy or treatment. There is no unemployment anymore. It's absurd that older people retire. Those are the ones with the most experience in their field. He who rests, rusts. We are able to learn and further educate ourselves our whole lives. Pension as we know it doesn't exist, there could be medical screening tests to see if and how much one is capable to practice his/her profession. It would be decided if they help in the company with advice and suggestions or work at home. There is a standard requirement of how much everybody works like nowadays a 36-40 hours week and 30 days holiday per year. The goal to achieve is that working hours get reduced so that everybody has more spare time. People that have children or have to nurse somebody can also do a part-time job. It's desirable that as little as possible is consumed, so that we save our environment from being exploited.

6. POINT SYSTEM

Everyone that cannot work like children, severely disabled, seniors and students get monthly credit on their card. The credit could be called Eco-Points for example 500 Eco-Points, with your points you pay your daily needs. People that work get on top of the 500 Eco-Points (EP) their salary paid, about 1000 EP. The Points you receive are used to buy food, pay mortgages, incidental rental costs, insurances, fuel etc. The goal is to spend as few Points as possible. At the end of the year the EP on the credit card could be calculated into spare time in days or hours, so the less Points you have spent the more spare time you get. An example: A man has a full-time job and earns 1500 EP, his wife works part-time and earns 1300 EP. Their 2 kids get 500 EP each, so the family has a monthly income of 3800 EP. Let's say 100 EP are worth 1 hour of spare time. The family was thrifty and at the end of the year, instead of the 45600 EP they only used up 36000 EP, so they have earned 96 hours or 12 work-days spare time. If you want/need to buy something bigger, than you go to the bank and they grant an installment payment. The cheapest products are those built ecologically, long-living and in the region. One could say that it's like our society nowadays and we could just stick with money. But it's a hugh difference if everybody works to earn more money and consume more goods, or if everyone works for more spare time. Companies and citizens can exchange EP in Euros or Dollars for example but the exchange rate is less than 1:1. Citizens who want to emigrate only get help from the state, if they move to another country with a Money Free Society.

7. FAMILY

Nowadays it's difficult to manage family and job at the same time. In former times usually the husband went to work and the wife took care of the children and did the house chores, which is now barely possible. To earn enough money you have to be flexible (2 or 3 jobs, long ways to work) and always available, which is negative for a harmonious family life. Parents have less time alone and latchkey kids are perfectly normal. In the Money Free Society (MFS) the family plays an important role and because everybody has more spare time, people can spend a lot of time and energy into their families and the children can have a good upbringing. In school, children should be taught about how to associate and communicate in the society and ecology, computer –and robot science are useful main subjects. Multigenerational houses and flat-sharing communities are more ecological because commodities and resources are used more efficiently and are therefore to be supported.

8. WORK

Companies don't compete in trying to make more products and increasing sales, but in making higher quality, ecological and regional goods. There should be a Department of the Environment that like a product testing foundation, tests all goods and service industries and then ascertain an approximate price range. The producers that make the best items (easy to repair) or offer the best services, get the cheapest EP rate. They are than consequently the most attractive manufacturers for consumers. For businesses that don't make any products or for those that offer free social services it would be advisable to insert EP wage agreements. The businesses that work the most environmental friendly could pay their workers minimal higher EP wages to give them an incentive to do even better. To employ the best workers for ones company, it is essential to improve in automation processes so that the employees can have more spare time. Being able to work at home is also a big advantage. Jobs that aren't very popular, for example where you have night –and holiday shifts could have minimal higher wages. There are so many inventions and alternative technologies that are environment friendly but not so profitable, like electric –and hydrogen motors, plastic made out of wood (biodegradable plastics) and recyclable –or returnable packaging that could be subsidized. Swap –and lending markets, carpools and carsharing would be more lucrative. Exported goods could be paid in monthly installments and have lifetime guarantees and would still be competitive because of their being best quality, sustainable, low consumption and highest technologically advanced. The generated money could be changed in EP and other countries that also have a MFS are the preferred trading partners. A business that has to import raw goods or products could get money from the bank if they have a sustainable concept that includes environmental aspects. In a MFS people try to repair things and not just throw them away, if something has to be replaced, than with a recyclable, long-living, biodegradable and highest technologically advanced spare part or whole product. Some lines of occupation and economic sectors are definitely going to disappear and make room for new jobs that will be created in the MFS. There would be less superrich and traffic, but it would be a win-win situation for the most of us. In the MFS, rich countries would have enough human resources because of automation and the extra pension and jobless new workers. The populations in poor countries wouldn't explode anymore because people enjoy social protection and are higher educated. We can try as hard as we can to reduce our ecological footprint, but if the world population continues to grow this fast, than we use up more resources and destroy Mother Earth.

9. HOUSING

Every citizen has a right to have a living space of approximately 30 square meters, so there are no more homeless. Everything above that is paid either by rent or paid off in installments. New houses and apartments should be built as environment friendly and low-energy as possible, solar roofs, thermal energy, solar collectors, wind turbines etc. are desirable. It is also profitable to grow your own organic vegetables and fruit or raise your own organic meat in your garden because you spend less EP and have more spare time. The goal is to have so low incidental rental costs as possible, so that you have more EP left at the end of the month.

10. FREE TIME

If you live and work environmentally conscious than you have more profit. On the contrary to capitalism, profit means more free time and not more money. We could call it otiumism instead of capitalism which means free time doctrine. But what should we do with more spare time? The answer is easy, everything that we don't have time to do now: Hobbies, progress yourself by joining a club, doing voluntary work, athletic activities or visiting events (music, art exhibitions). Or like mentioned before, you can grow your own food in a garden or in a producer organization and you could repair broken items, which both mean that you enjoy more free time. There should be free museum and trade fairs with workshops and round-table discussions, where people can experiment and discuss about how we can do everything more ecological and efficient. We would have more time to take care of and raise our children and enjoy family life. "Children are travelers, asking for the direction, let us be good advisors". We would be able to spend more time with friends and acquaintances and thanks to more relax and sleep, we would be less powered out and sick. You could talk with your boss or working team about how time is scheduled, which hours and days in the week have work in the company to be done and when you could work at home, like flexible working hours and a year free time "sabbaticals" would be easier to organize.

11. CLOSING REMARKS

A MFS without capitalism was not possible before, but because of the industrial revolutions, we have developed our world so far to the point that we can ask ourselves in what kind of world do we want to live in. If we continue to do things the way we do, than things are going to get worse and not better: More over-exploitation of natural resources, terror, refugees and environmental pollution, more sickness because of stress, additives, pesticides and genetic engineering and lower social – and environmental standards because of free trade agreements. We can see that capitalism is at an end. New money is pumped into the markets to try to stimulate the economy, but it only widens the gap between rich and poor. Soon democracy will have to make way for capitalism and to be better prepared against social conflicts the see-through man will be monitored more intensively. We can be more outraged about the daily flood of crisis, scandals and catastrophes and than go back to "business as usual" or we can do something about it.

 That would be like if humanity was racing in 100 cars on a hugh wide road next to each other. At one point the street gets so small that it leads to one building; a motorcycle store. In the middle of the store, there's a way to drive through with one motorcycle at a time. What would you do? Do you fully accelerate and crash into another car or would you rather smash into the building? Or you could try to stop all the cars and tell everybody to get out and take a motorbike and one after the other drive through the building. It's easier to say that the other drivers won't listen anyway and keep on driving, but wouldn't it be more meaningful to try to convince as many drivers as possible to switch over? The drivers with fast Ferraris and luxurious Rollsroyces will probably be the most toughest to convince to switch over to a motorcycle. Why should I trade my fancy car for a motorbike? But it doesn't matter what nationality or if you're rich or poor, we are all in the same boot. We can't just do everything as usual, because our planet is decaying and we only have one Mother Earth. It's necessary that a state starts with MFS because there have to be standard health, education and employment structures. Most of the western countries are ideal; they have a social market economy, are high tech and have a high foreign trade ratio. But who will be the pioneer? Who wants to leave a hugh dump behind for future generations? Don't we want our children and childrens children to inherit an intact ecosystem? It can't be changed overnight, but we could go down in history as the generation that changed the world at the right time in a positive direction. If more and more countries implement a MFS, than we can save our planet. I don't believe that we humans are, as it is claimed, born greedy. I think it's the system that makes us think we need more and more of everything. Money doesn't make us happy. We are shortly delighted when we buy something new, but the feeling is quickly gone. What makes us enduringly happy is good social ties, doing something useful with your life and being one with nature. I am convinced that in a MFS there would be less envy, violence, broken relationships, crime, war and environmental catastrophes. You think you are only one person and can't change anything, but we are all important. We should discuss about it, talk in Chatrooms and start a MFS political party in every country. Let us choose to live in a world where machines do the work and we thereby profit from more free time, where we live together and not in rivalry against each other and where we live as one with nature and the environment. It's not too late...

Index of sources

1. https://www.lernhelfer.de/schuelerlexikon (page 4)
2. https://de.m.wikipedia.org/wiki/Faschismus (page 4)
3. politik-lexikon.at/planwirtschaft (page 4)
4. https:/ago.immerda.ch/index2.php?option= (page 5)
5. " Denn eins ist sicher: Die Rente "
   Spiegel.de/wirtschaft/soziales/norbert-bluem... (page 8)
6. sprueche.woxikon.de/sprueche-zur-geburt/1714
   „Kinder sind Reisende die nach dem Weg fragen, wir wollen Ihnen gute Begleiter sein „ (page 21)
7. translation: Englisch Wörter-Buch Trautwein Wörterbuch
   © 1994 Genehmigte Ausgabe
8. www.linguee.de/deutsch-englisch/ueberset